MILAN TAKES A BOW

Written by Michelle Allen
Illustrated by Marissa Allen

Milan Takes A Bow!

Written by Michelle Allen
Illustrated Marissa Allen

© Copyright Michelle Allen and Marissa Allen 2020

All Rights Reserved.
No part of this book may be reproduced, scanned or transmitted in any forms, digital, audio or printed, without the expressed written consent of the author.
Pa-Pro-Vi Publishing: www.paprovipublishing.com

Dedication

To my sweet angel Milan Thalia' Allen who is the inspiration for this book. May you know that you were and always will be loved. My other heartbeats, Marissa Allen, your artistic spirit, and talent brought the pages to life, MelodyAnn Ellison for seeing my vision and encouraging me to stay focused, and McHale Allen for your willingness to listen and laugh as I processed my thoughts. My husband, Miles Allen who always had faith in me, undying support for this book and anything I dream of. My mother, Mildred Bivens, who has listened to my stories since I have put pen to paper as a child.

May we all get lost in a great book!

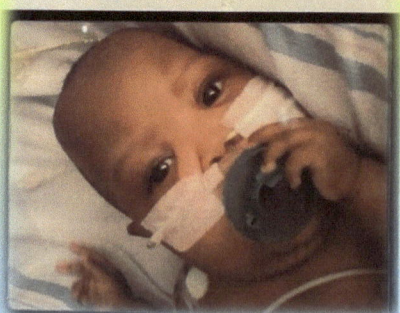

Contents

Rise and Shine

Breakfast

The Lesson

Practice

Help Arrives

Rise and Shine

Milan awakes from her slumber with the warmth of the sun on her face. She always loved how the sun seemed to dance on her walls and land on her bed. Milan was excited because she could smell "Mom's World-Famous French Toast" for breakfast. It was her absolute favorite, and she could not wait to add whipped cream on top. In fact, Mom always let her squeeze a little in her mouth before putting it on her food. Milan had better get downstairs before her sisters because they always raced to get the first slices. Milan was the youngest of three sisters and she had a little brother as well. She loved playing with "The Sibs" as they called themselves, but she valued her alone time for adventures. Milan has always had a vivid imagination. She often played dress up and loved to go to fun faraway places. But this day is special; it is unlike any day before. For today there is no pretending. Oh no! Milan has an important journey, and it will require practice and perfection. For today Milan is planning to meet the queen at the grand ball! But there is only one problem...Milan does not know how to take a bow...

Milan's excitement quickly turned to fear. She had forgotten to learn how to take a bow. She would look silly at the grand ball if she couldn't do it. Everyone would laugh at her. What could she do? She had an idea. She would learn to take a bow before the grand ball. If she practiced hard, she should have it. She didn't have time for breakfast because she had to get started right away. But how? Her Mom was calling her, and she knew she never miss Moms, World-Famous French Toast. But she may be disappointed finding out that she waited until the last minute to learn to take a bow…(Sigh) I better get downstairs and face the music.

Breakfast

Milan and her mother greeted each other with 'Good Morning' while her mother hurriedly placed two pieces of French toast in front of Milan. Milan's mother told her to enjoy her breakfast and that she would be right back after she checked on McHale.

Melody and Monet' had already beat her downstairs and got the first pieces of Mom's World-Famous French Toast. Monet' asks, "No whipped cream, Milan?" Milan playing with her food instead of eating it replied, "No, not today!" Everyone gasped, what? Are you sick? Melody screamed, "Mom Milan is sick, she never turns down whipped cream!" Monet' said, "No, don't call Mom, you know she's coming in full Momma Bear mode!" Milan quickly replied, "No I'm not sick, I just have a lot on my mind, I'll be fine!"

Monet' yelled, "Mom false alarm, Milan is not sick!" It was too late. Mom arrived with a utility belt that had all kinds of meds hanging from her waist. Aspirin, bandages, thermometer, ice pack, tummy ache and cold syrup. You name it. She had it! Monet' told her mother that it was a false alarm and apologized.

Mom left the kitchen. The girls huddled together and Monet' whispered, "Where did Mom get a cold icepack from? Ummmm we're all in the kitchen, but no one saw her get ice, who has an ice pack on demand?" Melody replied, "That's the Momma Bear in her, you know you can never hint to Mom that we are sick, she is magical." Puzzled, everyone had a great laugh, finished breakfast, and went about their day.

The Lesson

Milan really wanted to learn how to take a bow, instead she wasted time, lays across her bed and cries, but she knows she should really be practicing. Milan first decides what to wear. Got it! This gown is perfect! Then she decides what hairstyle she should have. Most importantly she decided who she would take to the grand ball that the Queen has invited her to. Well that was a no brainer. She would take her sisters Melody and Monet' only, because McHale hadn't quite mastered that potty training thingy yet. Besides, she surely didn't want to change training pants in her fancy dress. He's handsome…but not that handsome! At that moment Milan began to cry again. Monet' hears her and enters her room to find out why she is crying.

Monet asks, "What's wrong Milan? Is there any way I can help?" Milan with her eyes red from all of the crying looked at Monet' and responded, "You're going to think it's silly." Monet' responded, "I'm your big sister and I love you. I hate to see you crying. Come on. Trust me. I won't laugh." Milan with tears in her eyes quickly responds "Well...well..." Monet' yells, "My goodness Milan spit it out!" Milan blurts out, "Well...I'mGoingToAGrandBallAndIDon'tKnowHowToTakeABow! There I said it!!!" Then falls across the bed.

Monet', now using a softer voice asks, "Milan, please slow it down. I can't understand a word you are saying girl! I'm sorry for yelling but I want to help you!" Milan said she was sorry too then replied," I'm-going-to-a-grand-ball-and-I-don't-know-how-to-take-a-bow, WillYouHelpMe?" as she bats her eyes. Monet' responds, "The cute stuff usually doesn't work on me, but this is an emergency so I guess I will help. Let's get started."

Practice

Monet', not really sure how to bow herself, tries to show Milan how to take a bow. Surely she knows how to bow. Besides she's the big sister and big sisters know everything…Right? Monet' shouts, "Let us begin" and claps her hands twice (CLAP-CLAP!) now watch closely Milan this is quite easy. Monet' stands on her right leg with her left leg bent and said, "You bow like this!" But suddenly Monet' tips over and falls to the floor (THUMP!)

Milan said, "Now that doesn't look easy, but I'll try…" Monet' responds, "Yes, but leave the fall out and then you'll have it." Milan stands on her right leg, bends her left leg then falls over too (THUMP!).

They both agree that maybe they should try another way because it did not feel quite right. Monet' takes the lead and said "Okay, watch closely Milan, I really want you to get it this time. In fact, stand right in front and face me so we can do it together." Milan and Monet' stood in front of each other as Monet' talked them through the movements of the bow. Okay, this time stand on your left leg, bend your right leg, and lean forward. At that very moment they bumped heads (CLUNK!) followed by a huge (THUMP!) as they both fall to the floor.

Both girls shook their heads as if trying to shake off the pain and began to cry.

Monet' cried, "I'm sorry Milan I really thought I knew how to take a bow, but I guess I don't." Let's just take a break and practice again later.

Help Arrives

Melody hears all the thumping coming from upstairs and enters the room. "What are you guys doing? I can hear your thumping from downstairs!" This time, a very frustrated Monet' responds, "Well…We'reGoingToAGrandBallAndWeDon'tKnowHowToTakeABow! THUMP! They fall to the floor, again. "What? Girl slow it down! I don't understand what you're trying to say!" Melody demands. Again Monet' states, "Well…We're-Going-To-A-Grand-Ball-And-WE-Don't-Know-How-to-Take-A-Bow, CanYouHelpUs? "You mean all of that thumping was because you didn't know how to take a bow? You have got to be kidding."

"Well let me see what you've got!" Milan and Monet' got into position by standing in front of each other, stood on their right legs with the left leg bent and just as they were about to bump heads Melody screamed, "No wait! You two are going to hurt yourselves, no wonder there is so much thumping in here! Silly gooses, young ladies don't bow, they curtsy!" Milan asked, "What is a curtsy, and is it going to hurt? Because bowing sure does." "Of course not, it's amazingly easy" said Melody. They both pleaded, "Can you teach us? Because bowing hurts" while rubbing their heads. Melody said, "I will first show you how to curtsy then you can try it". Milan and Monet' jumped up and happily yelled, Okay! Melody was a pro at the art of curtsy because she had attended many grand balls. Melody then demonstrated the art of curtsy.

"Now you hold your dress about midway ever so gently in a pinch, lifting just a little to remain a lady then do a kind of a standing crisscross-apple sauce. Because it's the queen you want to bow your head a little, that's how you show respect to her royalness, and always...always have a pleasant look on your face, kind of a smile, but you don't have to show all your teeth. Now, do you think you both could do that?" Milan replied, "Yes, and it doesn't look painful either!" Milan and Monet' stood up, got into position and on the very first try they did a beautiful curtsy.

They both screamed, "We did it! We did it! Now we're ready to bow...I mean curtsy!" They all laughed. Melody then said, "Now that was perfect, I knew you would get it, you just needed to know how." Melody asked Monet', "Why didn't you simply ask for help?" Monet' responded, "I'on know, I guess I just got caught up in the big sister thing. Sorry Milan, next time I will ask for help when I am not sure of how to do things instead of pretending to know. It's just that I'm your big sister and I should have the answers when you come to me, but I now know it's okay to ask for help sometimes." Milan said, "That's ok, Monet' you were just trying to help."

The girls practiced for the rest of the day between trying on dresses for the queen's grand ball. They were so glad that Melody came when she did because they realized just how much they needed each other and learned that it is okay to ask for help." Now the girls are ready for the grand ball. I know, I know, you are wondering if Milan did the perfect curtsy at the grand ball before the queen. Hmmmmm, I guess you will have to find out when you read **"Milan and the Queens Grand Ball..."**

Until Then...

My Inspiration

Milan Thalia' Allen
November 3, 2006

Milan was born to Miles and Michelle Allen incredibly early at only 6 months, weighing a little over a pound. Tiny was an understatement. We knew her road would be challenging, but we were ready to fight for her life.

As a couple we banded together to ensure Milan had the absolute best care possible. As a family we ensured that she knew she was loved. We held her often and took numerous pictures to document her growth and progress. Family and friends sent well wishes of support and love to help us cope. Our forever family, the nurses charged with her care, loved us just as much as they loved her. We all quickly became friends and remain as such today. There were many sleepless nights, a lot of tears, several surgeries and hundreds of hours spent in hospital Neonatal Intensive Care Units (NICU). But all the love, prayers and medical treatment were not enough to sustain our sweet baby. At 10 ½ months Milan gained her wings and took her place as our Angel. Though devastated, we vowed to never forget her by keeping her in our prayers, our lives, and our hearts. Our son McHale who has never met his older sister knows that she was here.

Through this book Milan has a footprint in the world that is demonstrated through literature and art which depicts the little girl that stole our hearts. My prayer is if you have ever loss anyone close to you, I hope this helps because there is power is memories. To everyone that has ever lost a piece of their heart...I truly understand.

This is my story...What is yours?

About the Author

Michelle T. Allen is a Professor of Criminal Justice, and she is the author of the new children's book "Milan Takes A Bow". I know you are wondering how did she land on writing children's books? Easy children find the fun in unexpected situations.

Michelle has written, presented, and published scholarly works in higher education, but she is excited to share her fictional books aimed at bringing happiness to all children.

Michelle has been writing since the age of 12 and always wanted to be an Author. Later inspired by her children, she was happy to transition to writing children's books. Michelle was bitten by the children's book genre bug once she had taken a creative writing course in her undergraduate college studies. From that point she was hooked!

Michelle's degrees include an Associates in Liberal Arts, Bachelors in Sociology, Master of Science in Criminal Justice with a concentration in Critical Incident Management, Master of Philosophy in Criminal Justice and she is a candidate for a PhD in Criminal Justice with a concentration in Law and Public Policy. Michelle also, proudly serves as a member of
Alpha Kappa Alpha, Sorority Incorporated.

Michelle is motivated by her husband and children to give you the absolute best of her inner thoughts. Michelle captures the personality that she envisioned for Milan in the book as the daughter she longed to know. She hopes you enjoy her first book and will join her for many more to follow.

Michelle can be reached at: **mtallen12@gmail.com**

About the Illustrator

Marissa M. Allen is a college sophomore majoring in Elementary Education with a minor in Art. She is delighted to finally become an illustrator of her first children's book "Milan Takes A Bow!" Upon graduation she plans to teach art to special needs children while continuing her personal artistic endeavors. Marissa has been drawing since the age of 3 and has always dreamt of pursuing a career in the art world. In fact, she knew early on that art would be an integral part of her life. As her skill progressed, Marissa strived to master various art mediums such as: acrylic paint, watercolor, oil pastel, traditional sketches, and digital art. However, her favorites are sketching and digital art.

Marissa desires to dwell deeper into the world of children's literature and illustration and is excited to bring her little sisters' story to life in this very personal book.

Influenced by her loving family and sweet memories, Marissa creates her mothers' vision of the amazing little girl Milan could have been. Through this book she introduces the world to how she imagined Milan as a little sister. She is hopeful that you will be inspired by this journey.

Marissa can be reached at: **Blacklenses16@gmail.com**

www.ingramcontent.com/pod-product-compliance
Lightning Source LLC
Chambersburg PA
CBHW040100160426
43193CB00002B/33